BOOK
LUST

Journal

Featuring an Introduction and Recommendations by

NANCY PEARL

SASQUATCH BOOKS
SEATTLE

Printed in China
Published by Sasquatch Books
Distributed by Publishers Group West
14 13 12 11 10 09   10 9 8 7 6

Design by Rowan Moore/www.doublemranch.com

ISBN: 1-57061-453-9

Sasquatch Books
119 South Main Street, Suite 400
Seattle, WA 98104
(206) 467-4300
www.sasquatchbooks.com
custserv@sasquatchbooks.com

Introduction

There are only two regrets I have about a life devoted to reading. The first is that I'm sorry that I wasn't introduced to the novels of Iris Murdoch until the 1980s. I read all 26 of them, in no particular order, with a mixture of delight and awe, believing then, and still convinced now, that she was one of the most brilliant writers of the twentieth century. I know now that in all likelihood—time being short and the world of books growing ever larger—that I'll never have the time to go back and reread them. That's regret number one.

Regret number two is that I never kept track of the books that I have read. I would give almost anything to go back to being a kid and having a blank notebook in which I would write down the author and title of each book as I finished reading it. Certainly, early in the list would be Ruth Stiles Gannett's **My Father's Dragon;** Gertrude Chandler Warner's **The Boxcar Children;** and every horse and dog book in the library. Then would come the young adult novels—the Dinny Gordon series by Anne Emery and **Tradition**, another novel by Emery that introduced me to the plight of Japanese Americans during World War II; all the Betty Cavanna books; Robert Heinlein's **Space Cadet** and everything else by him; the Andre Norton novels; and so much more. I know I read those books (and now own many of them), but what about all the others that I know I loved but have forgotten? And what about all the books I've read as an adult? What treasures have I lost track of, all for the want of a notebook and the self-discipline to write it all down?

Well, finally, here's the notebook. It is divided into four sections: Book Notes, Book Passages to Remember, Books I Want to Read, and Books on Loan. Be responsible for your own self-discipline. Enjoy!

Nancy Pearl

THE RULE OF 50, OR,
ON NOT FINISHING A BOOK
YOU'VE BEGUN

One of my strongest-held beliefs is that no one should ever finish a book that they're not enjoying, no matter how popular or well reviewed the book is. Believe me, nobody is going to get any points in heaven by miserably slogging their way through a book they aren't enjoying but think they ought to read. I live by what I call "the rule of 50," which is based on the reality of the shortness of time and the immensity of the world of books. If you're 50 years old or younger, give every book about 50 pages before you decide to commit yourself to reading it, or give it up. If you're over 50, which is when time gets even shorter, subtract your age from 100—the result is the number of pages you should read before deciding. Factor into this an acknowledgment of how much your mood has to do with whether or not you will like a book. I always leave open the option of going back to a book that I haven't liked sometime later (especially if someone I respect has recommended it to me). I've begun many books (such as Matthew Kneale's **English Passengers**; John Crowley's **Little, Big**; and Andrea Barrett's **The Voyage of the Narwhal**), put them down without finishing, then returned a month or two—or years—later and ended up loving them.

THE PEARL 100

A List of Great Reads

Adventure by the Book, Nonfiction: Armchair travel readers are often also armchair adventure readers—it's far safer to sit at home and only dream of danger.

Fergus Fleming's	Barrow's Boys: A Stirring Story of Daring, Fortitude, and Outright Lunacy
Helen Whybrow's (editor)	Dead Reckoning: Great Adventure Writing from the Golden Age of Exploration, 1800–1900
Derek Lundy's	Godforsaken Sea: Racing the World's Most Dangerous Waters
Jon Krakauer's	Into Thin Air
Robert Byron's	The Road to Oxiana

Armchair Travel: Sometimes the best way to travel is across the room and into a comfortable chair, bringing along a cup of tea and a sense of adventure.

Dervla Murphy's	Full Tilt: Ireland to India with a Bicycle
Paul Theroux's	The Great Railway Bazaar
Bill Bryson's	Notes from a Small Island
Jonathan Raban's	Passage to Juneau
Eric Newby's	A Short Walk in the Hindu Kush

Authors Too Good to Miss: What else is there to say about these writers except that they produced (and in many cases continue to produce) great fiction.

Iris Murdoch

Richard Powers

Neal Stephenson

Rex Stout

Connie Willis

Best Fiction and Nonfiction about World War I: Perhaps it was the horrible realities of trench warfare, the wholesale slaughter of young men, or the changing role of women, but World War I was a particularly evocative war for writers.

Jeanne MacKenzie's	Children of the Souls
Patricia Anthony's	Flanders
Paul Fussell's	The Great War and Modern Memory
Dalton Trumbo's	Johnny Got His Gun
Pat Barker's	Regeneration

Best Novels with Dogs: There are some novels in which the dog, although maybe not the main character, steals the book.

Clifford Simak's	City
James Streeter's	Good-bye, My Lady
Paul Auster's	Timbuktu
Connie Willis's	To Say Nothing of the Dog
Thomas King's	Truth & Bright Water

Brothers and Sisters: Some of my favorite books are about the sometimes difficult, sometimes loving relationship between siblings.

David James Duncan's	The Brothers K
Anne Tyler's	Dinner at the Homesick Restaurant
Antonya Nelson's	Living to Tell
Susan Richards Shreve's	Plum & Jaggers
Josephine Hart's	The Reconstructionist

The Davids: Some of my favorite writers are linked only by the fact that they share the same first name.

David Leavitt's	The Body of Jonah Boyd
David Halberstam's	The Fifties
David Kirby's	The Ha-Ha

David Sedaris's Me Talk Pretty One Day
David Lodge's Small World

First Novels: I am very partial to first novels. There's something so hopeful about them—it's exciting to discover an author you adore right at the beginning of his or her career.

Elizabeth Strout's Amy and Isabelle
Ann Packer's The Dive from Clausen's Pier
Jonathan Safran Foer's Everything Is Illuminated
John Griesemer's No One Thinks of Greenland
John Derbyshire's Seeing Calvin Coolidge in a Dream

Friend-makers: There are some books that are so idiosyncratic that when you stumble across someone who has not only read but loved the book as much as you have, you know you've made a friend for life.

P. F. Kluge's Biggest Elvis
Clair Huffaker's The Cowboy and the Cossack
Frederick Dillen's Fool
Frederick Reuss's Horace Afoot
Jon Cohen's The Man in the Window

Go Ahead and Laugh Aloud: Some books make it impossible not to guffaw, roar, and laugh until you cry.

William Kotzwinkle's The Bear Went Over the Mountain
P. G. Wodehouse's Carry On, Jeeves
Roy Lewis's The Evolution Man, or, How I Ate My Father
Jerome K. Jerome's Three Men in a Boat (To Say Nothing of the Dog)
Peter De Vries's The Tunnel of Love

Historical Fiction: I remain convinced that the best way to learn history is to read an outstanding work of fiction.

Rosemary Sutcliff's	The Eagle of the Ninth
Dorothy Dunnett's	The Game of Kings
Esther Forbes's	Johnny Tremain
Paul Scott's	The Raj Quartet
Stephanie Plowman's	The Road to Sardis

Memoirs: A good memoir is like a good novel—well written and filled with three-dimensional characters.

Caroline Knapp's	Drinking: A Love Story
Haven Kimmel's	A Girl Named Zippy: Growing Up Small in Mooreland, Indiana
Mary Karr's	The Liars' Club
Robert M. Sapolsky's	A Primate's Memoir
Ann Patchett's	Truth & Beauty

Pawns of History: Sometimes characters in fiction are caught up in the larger events of their times, as in these terrific novels.

Chang-rae Lee's	A Gesture Life
Patricia Henley's	Hummingbird House
James Buchan's	The Persian Bride
Marge Piercy's	Vida
Marilyn French's	The Women's Room

Poetry for the People: Want to read some wonderful poems? Try the following writers.

Mary Oliver's	Blue Iris
Edna St. Vincent Millay's	Collected Poems
Stephen Dunn's	Different Hours: Poems
W. S. Merwin's	Flower & Hand: Poems 1977–1983
James Tate's	Shroud of the Gnome

Short Stories: V. S. Pritchett, a master of the format, said that "the novel tends to tell us everything, whereas the short story tells us only one thing, and that intensely."

T. C. Boyle's	After the Plague and Other Stories
Dan Chaon's	Among the Missing
Lorrie Moore's	Birds of America
Laurie Colwin's	The Lone Pilgrim
Nell Freudenberger's	Lucky Girls

Sisters: Birth order, men, career choices, competition, and rivalry all contribute to the sometimes fraught relationships of sisters.

Diana Abu-Jaber's	Arabian Jazz
Richard B. Wright's	Clara Callan
David Long's	The Falling Boy
Shirley Hazzard's	The Transit of Venus
Jincy Willett's	Winner of the National Book Award

Space Operas: Derring-do, adrenaline-pumping nonstop adventure, life-or-death situations, planets to save, galaxies to conquer—who could ask for more?

Richard Morgan's	Altered Carbon
Orson Scott Card's	Ender's Game
Joe Haldeman's	The Forever War
Peter F. Hamilton's	Pandora's Star
Lois McMaster Bujold's	Shards of Honor

Spies in Fiction: Although nonfiction about the world of spies and spycraft seems sometimes to be even more unreal than fiction does, here are some of my favorite novels.

Robert Littell's	The Company
Bryan Forbes's	The Endless Game
Charles McCarry's	The Miernik Dossier

John le Carré's   A Perfect Spy
Manning Coles's   Drink to Yesterday

Summer Reads: The best of these are light reads—nothing much to overtax your brain while you're lolling in a hammock, but at the same time entertaining enough to keep you involved.

Stephen McCauley's   The Easy Way Out
Melissa Bank's   The Girls' Guide to Hunting and Fishing
Lee Child's   Killing Floor
Marian Keyes's   The Other Side of the Story
Richard Russo's   Straight Man

Wild Life: Our experiences with the natural world and animals, insects, and other creatures make for some wonderful reading.

Craig Childs's   Crossing Paths:
Uncommon Encounters with Animals
in the Wild

David Quammen's   Monster of God:
The Man-Eating Predator in the Jungles of
History and the Mind

Jonathan Weiner's   The Beak of the Finch:
A Story of Evolution in Our Time

Sharman Apt Russell's   An Obsession with Butterflies:
Our Long Love Affair with a Singular Insect

Lyanda Lynn Haupt's   Rare Encounters with Ordinary Birds

BOOK

NOTES

TITLE:

AUTHOR: **DATE:**

Notes/Comments:

TITLE:

AUTHOR: **DATE:**

Notes/Comments:

TITLE:

AUTHOR: **DATE:**

Notes/Comments:

TITLE:

AUTHOR: **DATE:**

Notes/Comments:

TITLE:

AUTHOR: **DATE:**

Notes/Comments:

TITLE:

AUTHOR: **DATE:**

Notes/Comments:

TITLE:

AUTHOR: **DATE:**

Notes/Comments:

TITLE:

AUTHOR: **DATE:**

Notes/Comments:

TITLE:

AUTHOR: **DATE:**

Notes/Comments:

TITLE:

AUTHOR: **DATE:**

Notes/Comments:

TITLE:

AUTHOR: **DATE:**

Notes/Comments:

TITLE:

AUTHOR: **DATE:**

Notes/Comments:

TITLE:

AUTHOR: **DATE:**

Notes/Comments:

TITLE:

AUTHOR: **DATE:**

Notes/Comments:

TITLE:

AUTHOR: **DATE:**

Notes/Comments:

TITLE:

AUTHOR: **DATE:**

Notes/Comments:

TITLE:

AUTHOR: **DATE:**

Notes/Comments:

TITLE:

AUTHOR: DATE:

Notes/Comments:

TITLE:

AUTHOR: **DATE:**

Notes/Comments:

TITLE:

AUTHOR: **DATE:**

Notes/Comments:

TITLE:

AUTHOR: **DATE:**

Notes/Comments:

TITLE:

AUTHOR: DATE:

Notes/Comments:

TITLE:

AUTHOR: DATE:

Notes/Comments:

TITLE:

AUTHOR: **DATE:**

Notes/Comments:

TITLE:

AUTHOR: **DATE:**

Notes/Comments:

TITLE:

AUTHOR: **DATE:**

Notes/Comments:

TITLE:

AUTHOR: **DATE:**

Notes/Comments:

TITLE:

AUTHOR: **DATE:**

Notes/Comments:

TITLE:

AUTHOR: **DATE:**

Notes/Comments:

TITLE:

AUTHOR: **DATE:**

Notes/Comments:

TITLE:

AUTHOR: **DATE:**

Notes/Comments:

TITLE:

AUTHOR: **DATE:**

Notes/Comments:

TITLE:

AUTHOR: **DATE:**

Notes/Comments:

TITLE:

AUTHOR: **DATE:**

Notes/Comments:

TITLE:

AUTHOR: **DATE:**

Notes/Comments:

TITLE:

AUTHOR: **DATE:**

Notes/Comments:

TITLE:

AUTHOR: DATE:

Notes/Comments:

TITLE:

AUTHOR: **DATE:**

Notes/Comments:

TITLE:

AUTHOR: **DATE:**

Notes/Comments:

TITLE:

AUTHOR: **DATE:**

Notes/Comments:

TITLE:

AUTHOR: **DATE:**

Notes/Comments:

TITLE:

AUTHOR: **DATE:**

Notes/Comments:

TITLE:

AUTHOR: **DATE:**

Notes/Comments:

TITLE:

AUTHOR: **DATE:**

Notes/Comments:

TITLE:

AUTHOR: **DATE:**

Notes/Comments:

TITLE:

AUTHOR: **DATE:**

Notes/Comments:

TITLE:

AUTHOR: **DATE:**

Notes / Comments:

TITLE:

AUTHOR: **DATE:**

Notes/Comments:

TITLE:

AUTHOR: **DATE:**

Notes/Comments:

TITLE:

AUTHOR: **DATE:**

Notes/Comments:

TITLE:

AUTHOR: DATE:

Notes/Comments:

TITLE:

AUTHOR: **DATE:**

Notes/Comments:

TITLE:

AUTHOR: **DATE:**

Notes/Comments:

TITLE:

AUTHOR: **DATE:**

Notes/Comments:

TITLE:

AUTHOR: **DATE:**

Notes/Comments:

TITLE:

AUTHOR:　　　　　　　　　　　　　　　　　　**DATE:**

Notes/Comments:

BOOK

PASSAGES TO REMEMBER

(including great first lines)

BOOKS

I WANT TO READ

TITLE: **AUTHOR:**

Synopsis:

How did I hear about this?

TITLE: **AUTHOR:**

Synopsis:

How did I hear about this?

TITLE: **AUTHOR:**

Synopsis:

How did I hear about this?

TITLE: **AUTHOR:**

Synopsis:

How did I hear about this?

TITLE: **AUTHOR:**

Synopsis:

How did I hear about this?

TITLE: **AUTHOR:**

Synopsis:

How did I hear about this?

TITLE: **AUTHOR:**

Synopsis:

How did I hear about this?

TITLE: **AUTHOR:**

Synopsis:

How did I hear about this?

TITLE: AUTHOR:

Synopsis:

How did I hear about this?

TITLE: AUTHOR:

Synopsis:

How did I hear about this?

TITLE: AUTHOR:

Synopsis:

How did I hear about this?

TITLE: AUTHOR:

Synopsis:

How did I hear about this?

TITLE: **AUTHOR:**

Synopsis:

How did I hear about this?

TITLE: **AUTHOR:**

Synopsis:

How did I hear about this?

TITLE: **AUTHOR:**

Synopsis:

How did I hear about this?

TITLE: **AUTHOR:**

Synopsis:

How did I hear about this?

TITLE: **AUTHOR:**

Synopsis:

How did I hear about this?

TITLE: **AUTHOR:**

Synopsis:

How did I hear about this?

TITLE: **AUTHOR:**

Synopsis:

How did I hear about this?

TITLE: **AUTHOR:**

Synopsis:

How did I hear about this?

TITLE: **AUTHOR:**

Synopsis:

How did I hear about this?

TITLE: **AUTHOR:**

Synopsis:

How did I hear about this?

TITLE: **AUTHOR:**

Synopsis:

How did I hear about this?

TITLE: **AUTHOR:**

Synopsis:

How did I hear about this?

TITLE: AUTHOR:

Synopsis:

How did I hear about this?

TITLE: AUTHOR:

Synopsis:

How did I hear about this?

TITLE: AUTHOR:

Synopsis:

How did I hear about this?

TITLE: AUTHOR:

Synopsis:

How did I hear about this?

TITLE: AUTHOR:

Synopsis:

How did I hear about this?

TITLE: AUTHOR:

Synopsis:

How did I hear about this?

TITLE: AUTHOR:

Synopsis:

How did I hear about this?

TITLE: AUTHOR:

Synopsis:

How did I hear about this?

BOOKS

ON LOAN

TITLE: **AUTHOR:**

Loaned out to: `ON`   *Returned:*

TITLE: **AUTHOR:**

Loaned out to: `ON`   *Returned:*

TITLE: **AUTHOR:**

Loaned out to: `ON`   *Returned:*

TITLE: **AUTHOR:**

Loaned out to: `ON`   *Returned:*

TITLE: **AUTHOR:**

Loaned out to: `ON`   *Returned:*

TITLE: **AUTHOR:**

Loaned out to: `ON`   *Returned:*

TITLE: **AUTHOR:**

Loaned out to: `ON`   *Returned:*

TITLE: **AUTHOR:**

Loaned out to: `ON`   *Returned:*

TITLE: | **AUTHOR:**

Loaned out to: | **ON** | *Returned:* ⬜

TITLE: | **AUTHOR:**

Loaned out to: | **ON** | *Returned:* ⬜

TITLE: | **AUTHOR:**

Loaned out to: | **ON** | *Returned:* ⬜

TITLE: | **AUTHOR:**

Loaned out to: | **ON** | *Returned:* ⬜

TITLE: | **AUTHOR:**

Loaned out to: | **ON** | *Returned:* ⬜

TITLE: | **AUTHOR:**

Loaned out to: | **ON** | *Returned:* ⬜

TITLE: | **AUTHOR:**

Loaned out to: | **ON** | *Returned:* ⬜

TITLE: | **AUTHOR:**

Loaned out to: | **ON** | *Returned:* ⬜

TITLE: AUTHOR:

Loaned out to: ON *Returned:*

TITLE: AUTHOR:

Loaned out to: ON *Returned:*

TITLE: AUTHOR:

Loaned out to: ON *Returned:*

TITLE: AUTHOR:

Loaned out to: ON *Returned:*

TITLE: AUTHOR:

Loaned out to: ON *Returned:*

TITLE: AUTHOR:

Loaned out to: ON *Returned:*

TITLE: AUTHOR:

Loaned out to: ON *Returned:*

TITLE: AUTHOR:

Loaned out to: ON *Returned:*

TITLE: **AUTHOR:**

Loaned out to: `ON`   *Returned:*

TITLE: **AUTHOR:**

Loaned out to: `ON`   *Returned:*

TITLE: **AUTHOR:**

Loaned out to: `ON`   *Returned:*

TITLE: **AUTHOR:**

Loaned out to: `ON`   *Returned:*

TITLE: **AUTHOR:**

Loaned out to: `ON`   *Returned:*

TITLE: **AUTHOR:**

Loaned out to: `ON`   *Returned:*

TITLE: **AUTHOR:**

Loaned out to: `ON`   *Returned:*

TITLE: **AUTHOR:**

Loaned out to: `ON`   *Returned:*

TITLE:　　　　　　　　　　　　　　　　**AUTHOR:**

Loaned out to:　　　　　　ON　　　　　*Returned:*

TITLE:　　　　　　　　　　　　　　　　**AUTHOR:**

Loaned out to:　　　　　　ON　　　　　*Returned:*

TITLE:　　　　　　　　　　　　　　　　**AUTHOR:**

Loaned out to:　　　　　　ON　　　　　*Returned:*

TITLE:　　　　　　　　　　　　　　　　**AUTHOR:**

Loaned out to:　　　　　　ON　　　　　*Returned:*

TITLE:　　　　　　　　　　　　　　　　**AUTHOR:**

Loaned out to:　　　　　　ON　　　　　*Returned:*

TITLE:　　　　　　　　　　　　　　　　**AUTHOR:**

Loaned out to:　　　　　　ON　　　　　*Returned:*

TITLE:　　　　　　　　　　　　　　　　**AUTHOR:**

Loaned out to:　　　　　　ON　　　　　*Returned:*

TITLE:　　　　　　　　　　　　　　　　**AUTHOR:**

Loaned out to:　　　　　　ON　　　　　*Returned:*

TITLE: **AUTHOR:**

Loaned out to: **ON**   *Returned:*

TITLE: **AUTHOR:**

Loaned out to: **ON**   *Returned:*

TITLE: **AUTHOR:**

Loaned out to: **ON**   *Returned:*

TITLE: **AUTHOR:**

Loaned out to: **ON**   *Returned:*

TITLE: **AUTHOR:**

Loaned out to: **ON**   *Returned:*

TITLE: **AUTHOR:**

Loaned out to: **ON**   *Returned:*

TITLE: **AUTHOR:**

Loaned out to: **ON**   *Returned:*

TITLE: **AUTHOR:**

Loaned out to: **ON**   *Returned:*